SMALL
Living

SMALL
Living

LOFT

Idea and concept: Paco Asensio

Editor and original texts: Sandra Moya

English translation: Antonio Moreno

Art direction: Mireia Casanovas Soley

Graphic design and layout: Ignasi Gracia Blanco

2006 © LOFT Publications

Via Laietana 32, 4º Of. 92

08003 Barcelona, Spain

Tel.: +34 932 688 088

Fax: +34 932 687 073

loft@loftpublications.com

www.loftpublications.com

ISBN 10: 84-95832-78-X

ISBN 13: 978-84-95832-78-8

Printed and bound in China

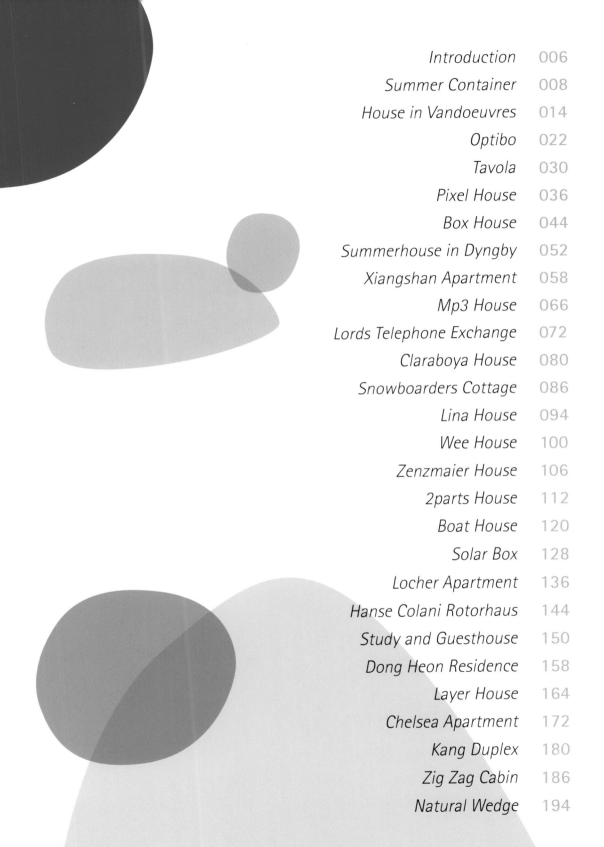

Introduction	006
Summer Container	008
House in Vandoeuvres	014
Optibo	022
Tavola	030
Pixel House	036
Box House	044
Summerhouse in Dyngby	052
Xiangshan Apartment	058
Mp3 House	066
Lords Telephone Exchange	072
Claraboya House	080
Snowboarders Cottage	086
Lina House	094
Wee House	100
Zenzmaier House	106
2parts House	112
Boat House	120
Solar Box	128
Locher Apartment	136
Hanse Colani Rotorhaus	144
Study and Guesthouse	150
Dong Heon Residence	158
Layer House	164
Chelsea Apartment	172
Kang Duplex	180
Zig Zag Cabin	186
Natural Wedge	194

New trends, new designs, new decorative lines... A lot of things have evolved and adapted to our changing lifestyles. Homes, and more specifically, their interior design, have evolved as well.

Our homes have to be comfortable, and today's pace reduces the amount of time we spend there. That is why you have to create a relaxed, intimate, cozy atmosphere that adapts to our individual tastes, helping us get away and leave behind everything that was stressing us out throughout the day. And it's as the French writer Ernest Renan said: "The truth of Gods was in proportion to the solid beauty of the temples reared in their honor." A house says a lot about its owner. By looking at its style, arrangement, decoration and even its tinier details we can tell what the person who lives there is like and that's crucial. You have to give a home personality, your personality, to make it unique and different from the rest.

But despite our quest for that which is comfortable and esthetically pretty we mustn't ignore one of the most basic characteristics all homes should have: practicality. Sure we should decorate the rooms according to our taste, sure we should use those colors which please us most... But one should never forget that a house has to serve certain purposes.

That's what this book is about, combining beauty with practicality, and more importantly, how to achieve these two objectives in small spaces, which are increasingly more common wherever housing is concerned. We'll see how in 355 square feet houses such as the Solar Box, glass becomes a key element for making the most out of the solar light for as long as possible or how using made to measure furniture, solves the question of how to adapt interiors to smaller spaces, see the Snowboarders Cottage. The idea is to find practical solutions for the space available and see to it that today's designs and latest trends are reflected in it.

"Architecture should be carnal, substantial, both spiritually and speculatively but with no other choice than to adapt to the space." This quote by the French-Swiss architect Le Corbusier, widely considered the most important in modern architecture, sums up best what you'll find in the following pages.

Summer Container > 388 sq. ft.

Markku Hedman

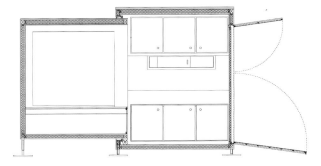

Elevations

In recent years design has made the great evolution in home construction possible. We're looking at a mobile home, a house we can move form one place to another and enjoy throughout our holidays. It's what is referred to as a caravan, but in this case it's not a conventional caravan like the ones we're used to seeing. This home strays from the structure you typically find in those kinds of homes.

We're looking at a wood cube that is easy to transport and once it is installed where we want it, it opens itself to its surroundings by way of its windows.

This time we're not talking about large windows to view the landscape, its small openings are perfect for their main objective: airing out the small home and allowing the necessary light to come through.

When mentioning its small windows we must speak about the real purpose of this home. It is a small residence that only provides the basic necessities; it's not made with the idea of spending most of your day inside. It's only used for eating and sleeping. That's why the interior décor is simple, devoid of eccentricities and impossible designs.

Wood predominates inside to give the room a rustic feel that is in touch with nature; and on the outside, because it is a light material, easy to transport from one place to another.

The doors and windows close with wood shutters, giving the caravan a touch of uniformity.

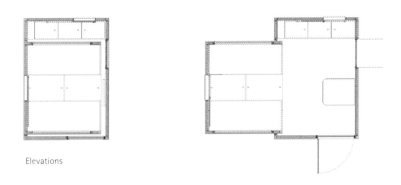

Elevations

House in Vandoeuvres > 248 sq. ft.

Charles Pictet Architect
© Francesca Giovanelli/Geneva, Switzerland

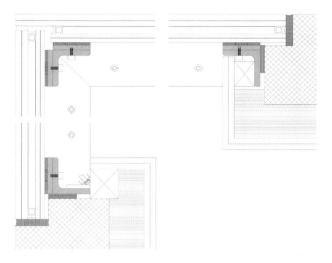

Floor plan

Buildings that serve as complements to the main home can choose whether to follow its structure and style or, to the contrary, be independent and not have any element connecting it to the main. Such is the case of the House in Vandoeuvres.

A giant block of stone in the middle of the yard suggests that we won't find anything related to the main house inside of it. It is an independent room to be used specifically as a private office.

As we said, it looks like a giant stone. The architect built it to connect the room with nature. Besides, it's a material that stands out for its great resistance to external elements, as well as to the passing of time, not to mention that it's easy to maintain.

But you have to give this giant block of stone a touch of modernity and distinction, and to do this they've used glass, another of the most recurring materials in construction. In this case, the large opaque windows predominate, allowing for natural light to come into the room throughout the day, but at the same time, keep people outside from seeing what's inside, giving the room a fair deal of privacy.

As far as its interior is concerned, its decoration depends on the use it will have. Since it will be an office, we have to make sure it is well lit. It's best to choose light colors for the walls because it will make the room brighter.

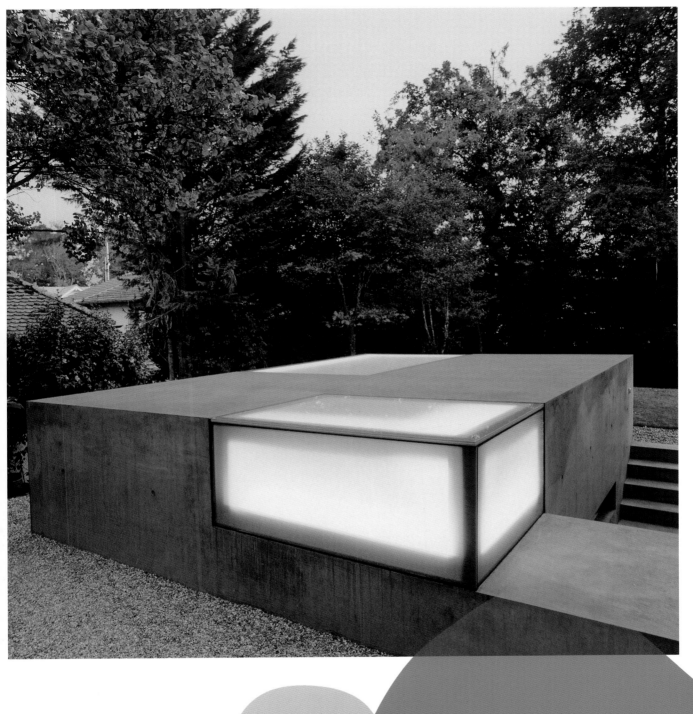

Despite being a giant block of stone it complements perfectly with the nature around it thanks to its color and the shade of its glass.

Elevation

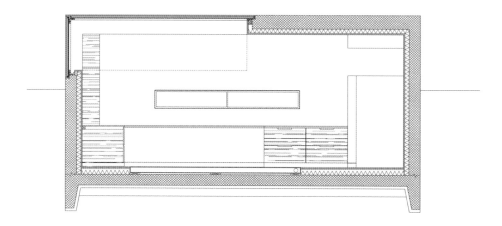

Section

Optibo > 270 sq. ft.

Shite Architects, White Design

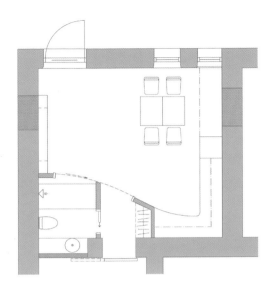

Floor plan

The lack of space and urban expansion augurs a future in which most houses will be on a small scale. Optibo is an original concept that makes it possible to enjoy an uncramped home in only 270 square feet. The secret lies in adapting the space to the use required at any particular time. Some pieces of furniture can be lowered and hidden in the floor, using an electric hydraulic system: the dining table and bed can appear or disappear as needed. One of the main assets of Optibo is its use of technology and materials that respect the environment, such as fiber optics and LED for the lighting. This prototype was designed in accordance with the Agenda 21 program, adopted by the UN at its conference in Rio de Janeiro in 1992.

The electric hydraulic system makes it possible to
effortlessly raise or lower the bed and table; the
technological resources available also allow to graduate
the height of the furniture or the intensity of the light.
This adaptation of the space makes it possible to achieve
comfort and expansiveness.

Tavola > 840 sq. ft.

Milligram Studio
© Takeshi Taira/Saitama, Japan

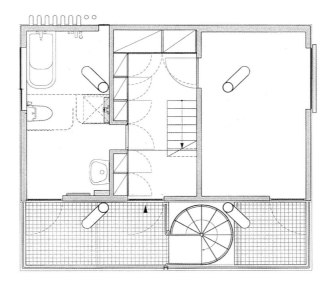

Floor plan

It seems that Japanese engineers' imagination is always a step ahead of that of the rest of the world. Who else would think of raising a home a few meters above the ground with an iron structure? By doing this they maximize a small space, not to mention using metal as a fundamental element clearly makes for a fresh and modern image. A construction such as this one stands out from the buildings around it, giving it a unique touch that is different from anything you might have seen before. Besides, metal is a resistant material that perfectly withstands serving as the foundation for a home.

As for the interior, what do you have to do to make a small space seem more spacious? The most important is to be sure about what you really need. You have to avoid overloading the home with elements that aren't necessary, whether they are decorative or not. Your choice of wall color also helps in this sense.

In this case, white predominates. It's a bright color that gives a sense of depth, favoring the effect of the natural light. As far as lamps are concerned, we should steer clear of large and ostentatious ones that take up too much space. It's best is to use halogens and spotlights. They are perfect for small spaces, giving off a clean and direct light that, together with the white walls, makes our room even larger.

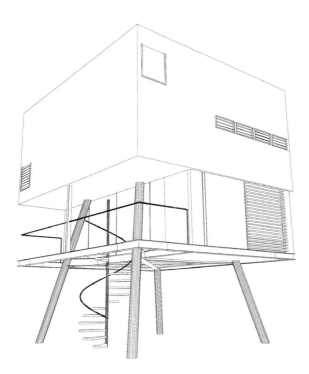

Perspective

Minimalist decoration is the best for small spaces. What's more, searching for contrast between the wall tones and the decorative elements makes for a more hip and modern design.

Pixel House > 915 sq. ft.

Slade Architecture & Mass Studies

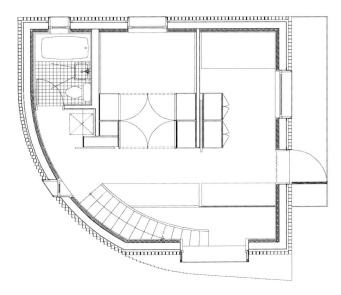

Floor plan

When finishing a home, the most common thing is to cover the bricks, a material frequently used in apartment and house construction. But it's not always the case, as we can see in the Pixel House. Why? One of the reasons is because we don't find it right in the city-center. It's built in an open area surrounded by natural elements, which is why leaving the bricks visible is more common.

But the most interesting thing about them is how they have been placed. It's as if they were small points that when they come together make for a place where one can actually live. Hence the name, since arranging bricks in this manner resembles the pixels found in digital images.

As we said before, it is located in an open area, which allows its inhabitants to enjoy the area to its fullest, with a large area of level ground surrounding the house.

This contact with nature is also evident when we step inside. Wood predominates, where light tones perfectly comple-ment the large windows communicating the house with the outdoors, and achieving an atmosphere that is in close contact with nature.

Its large windows make it possible for the home to be connected to the outdoors in such a manner that they mutually complement each other.

Halogen lights are best in areas with curved lines. They are small lights that adapt to spaces without problems and give the perfect light.

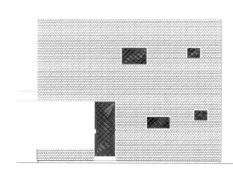

Elevation

Elevation

Box House > 538 sq. ft.

Nicholas Murcutt/Nelson Murcutt Architects

© Brett Boardman/Tathra, Australia

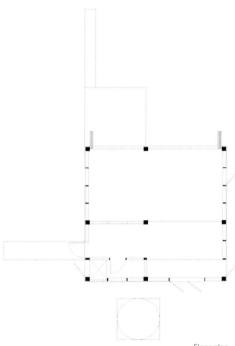

Floor plan

While earlier we were looking at a mobile caravan (see "Summer Container") here we'll pick up again on this concept but this time we have a static caravan. This allows the home to be larger, more spacious.

The first thing that calls our attention is that the structure rests on nine steel pillars, despite being built on a large level piece of land. This gives the home a modern touch because it strays from conventionality come time for construction. They wanted to make the home unique; to give it a modern look without sacrificing the connection you should have between a home and its immediate environment. In addition, by choosing to use pillars the architect improves the views you'd have from the inside.

Since it is a seasonal home where we'd only spend a given amount of time, it doesn't have the commodities we'd have in our daily home. That is why in this home the most important thing is that it opens up to the outdoors so we can enjoy it to its fullest. Hence the predominance of windows. But not all of them are the same, they serve different purposes. The main facade is practically entirely made of glass, thus improving the natural light while assuring an impressive view. On another side we find the rear and side windows with the purpose of airing out the home, without forgetting their decorative purpose.

The use of wood on the interior and exterior give it a classic touch, it is a material that never goes out of style, and it's modern thanks to the way it has been combined with glass.

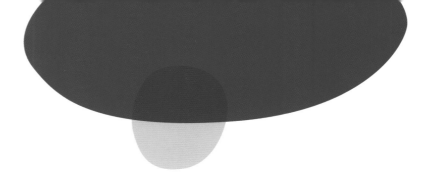

Elevations

Summerhouse in Dyngby > 936 sq. ft.

Claus Hermansen
© Anders Kavin/Jylland, Denmark

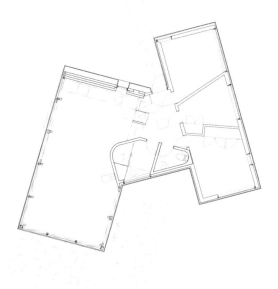

Floor plan

Even at first sight this house has everything you need to see that it's in a great position to be occupied. It has a conventional structure; located on a large area of level ground, which means that it didn't have to adapt to any geographical anomalies. What can we highlight about this home? It's "wrapping". Its base is concrete but the architect wanted to break away from its usual appearance and give it a personal touch with some rock wool.

It's a material that is rarely used but the truth is it has lots of advantages. Its placement is good for isolating heat or cold, in other words it's a multidirectional structure that thermically isolates homes, making the temperature inside better, not to mention it saves a considerable amount of energy.

Besides thermically isolating and fighting excessive noise, rock wool has easy maintenance and lasts a very long time. It is impermeable, meaning it can handle water, and it fights humidity. One final, but not less important, detail is that it withstands heat. It is capable of handling up to 1,832 °F meaning it is an incombustible material that doesn't generate toxic gases or smoke, making it fundamental in constructions where there is a risk of fire.

The climbing plants soften the structure's straight lines and visually connect the interior with the surroundings.

Elevation

Xiangshan Apartment

Hank M. Chao/Mohen Design

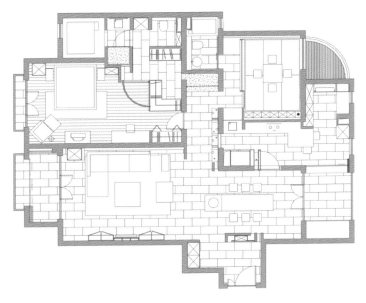

Floor plan

This apartment stands out for its elegance, for having a timeless décor and because the combination of materials manage to give the room an air of modernity.

It's curious to see dark colors predominating in a large space with windows, since these colors normally give off coldness but, at the same time, give the house a distinguishing touch. The coldness it produces is counterbalanced by small touches: choosing wood for the furniture adds a sense of relaxation and naturalness; placing simple curtains allow us to connect with the out-doors whenever we want, thus achieving that the house in integrated with its surroundings; and playing with lights to the benefit of our own personal well-being by placing small lamps in just the right places so as to only light the areas we wish.

We also have to highlight the surfaces used for both the walls and floor. If we focus in on it we see stone predominates, more specifically, granite. Stone represents its contact with nature and it's one of the few materials that are as good for flooring as it is for surfaces. The stones that are most commonly used are marble and slate but... Why did the architect choose granite ? Because it is much easier to maintain thanks to its great resistance to water and chemical cleaning products.

From the entrance, a rough metal wall acting as wardrobe
invites one inside; the private space here is separated
from the public by an interior bamboo garden that is
dramatically illuminated from the floor.

Mp3 House > 1,507 sq. ft.

Michel Rojkind & Simon Hamui

Mexico DF, Mexico

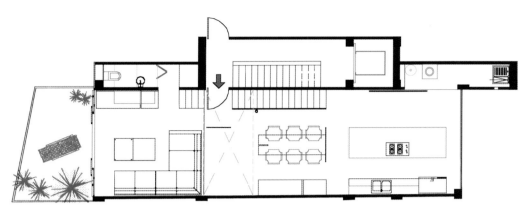

Floor plan

In a home with few openings to the outdoors, light is the most important element since it is what will give the home its personal touch, distinguishing it from the rest. In this case we're looking at a two-storey apartment, where the ground floor only connects with the outdoors by way of a small porch, and the rest of the rooms on this floor are closed off to the outdoors. That is why we find lots of halogen lights, which give off plenty of light without taking up much space and make the place look much more spacious. As far as the second floor goes, which is where we find the bedrooms and more private rooms, here we do see more windows and large windows dominating the living room. The fact that there is more natural light on this floor connects the house better with its surroundings.

As for the material used come time for decorating, once again wood predominates. As we mentioned earlier, the fact that there aren't many windows makes the home colder but thanks to the use of wood, this sensation disappears because it makes the house a lot more comfortable. This is also achieved if we opt for pastel colors come time for painting the walls.

This combination of materials, colors and furniture help create a modern home. For this reason, it's best to settle on a minimalist décor.

The distribution of open levels heightens the sensation of
space, visually connecting the different areas and making
the living space more dynamic.

Lords Telephone Exchange

Paskin Kyriakides Sands Architects
© Paskin Kyriakides Sands Architects/London, United Kingdom

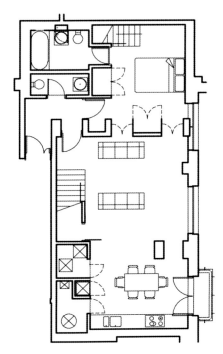

Floor plan

Large, bright apartments with all the commodities... That's what we're looking at here. Right from the start this home comes across as ideal because it includes all the elements that are characteristic of a house.

The first thing we have to highlight is the large window that governs over the living room. It maximizes the amount of time with natural light, connects the home with the outdoors, and allows us to enjoy the landscape around us without ever giving up our intimacy thanks to curtains and blinds that we'll put according to our taste. But this large window isn't enough for the architect, and to make the home appear even larger and cleaner, he opted to paint the walls white, and make great use of light color wood for the furniture. Furniture that takes good advantage of the space available, and that's why we see built-in closets that are made to measure and adapt to wherever we wish.

If we go upstairs we'll find the bedrooms, which we should point out are open, that is to say we can see them from downstairs thanks to the glass. This is a material that often isn't valued enough but is a key element that we find in almost every home, and which gives the distinctive touch to a home regardless of the decorative style we choose afterwards.

The original structure of this building was ideal for creating urban living spaces on multiple levels, resulting in the creation of a series of unique, modern apartments.

Building elevation

Claraboya House > 840 sq. ft.

Flemming Skude
© Flemming Skude/Lolland, Denmark

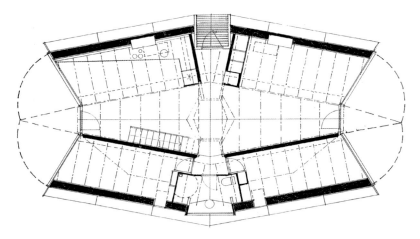

Floor plan

We've already seen inclined roofs on previous houses (see "Snowboarders Cottage") but this time its function is basically decorative. The center of the construction is marked by a large glass structure reminiscent of a triangle. This glass structure is positioned right in the middle so the solar light covers the entire place, giving good lighting and, at the same time, allowing for a perfect ventilation.

But what most calls our attention are its sides. They are built using large steel panels, a material that is resistant to the passing of time and meteorological effects and which, in addition, is easy and inexpensive to maintain. This type of structure makes it practically impossible for light to come in through the sides, which is why the architect decided to put the glass in the center. But we should also mention how the main facade is designed, after all, they continue using steel beside the entrance. Its placement is different, however. This allows natural light to enter but at the same time preserves the intimacy of the people living inside. With regards to the interior, the light effect produced by the steel panels makes us have to think carefully about how we're going to distribute the different spaces. There are two floors and we have to be sure about what we put at the highest level because this is where there will be most light.

Steel is a material that is often associated with coldness.
To break away from this image, it's best to choose wood
for the interior and give it a warmer touch.

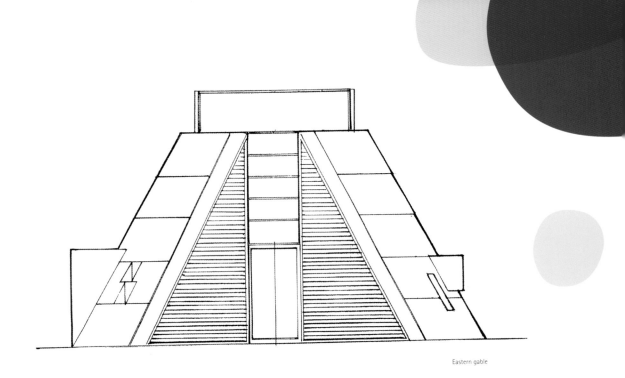

Eastern gable

Snowboarders Cottage > 689 sq. ft.

Ivan Kroupa

© Martin Rezabek, Libor Jebavy, Ivan Kroupa/Herlikovice, Czech Republic

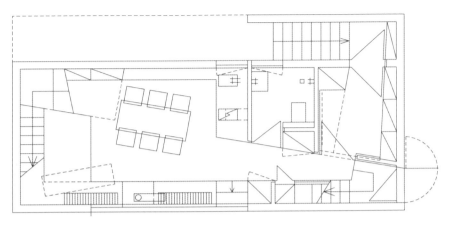

Floor plan

Once again we're looking at a kind of home that's been built for relaxation, to spend a few days away from the daily routine. This cabin was built to be used mainly in winter, more specifically, when the ski slopes are open. It's a small cabin but with all the basic necessities to spend a few restful days (in constructions like these we just take it for granted that electricity is not one of those necessities). And since it couldn't be any other way, the house is perfectly integrated with its environment.

As far as its exterior structure is concerned, the thing that stands out most is its roof, which follows the mountain's natural inclination. What did the architect have in mind? He just wanted to protect the place. Because it was built on the middle of the mountain, in an area where hard rain and snow is common, the best thing is to put a roof like this so water runs down the mountain.

As for its interior, it is fundamental to achieve a warm and natural atmosphere where we can relax. Once again, wood is the best material for this, but that doesn't mean we can't use color. The furniture, which has been made to measure, adapts perfectly to the dimensions of the place, and by giving it a touch of color we personalize the space and make it unique.

In this case the windows are basically decorative. The small porch allows them to enjoy the area right outside the house.

Section

Lina House > 635 sq. ft.

Caramel Architekten
© Caramel Architekten/Linz, Austria

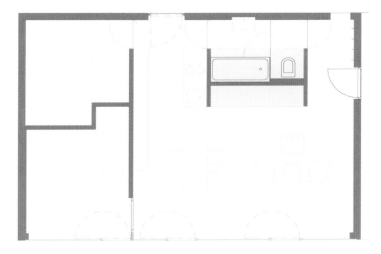

Floor plan

This home was built as complementary to the main home but it is not an extension, that is to say it doesn't follow its structure. We're looking at a mobile home consisting of a single module, placed by necessity and which easily solves the question of a home.

What we just said is one of the main advantages of a mobile home, but not the only one. These types of homes perfectly meet the needs of their inhabitants because they are built quickly. The house adapts to what we wish, instead of being us who must adapt to what the home offers. But in addition to these most noteworthy characteristics, we should also mention how easy it is to build these kinds of homes. They can be built anywhere, without needing to adapt to the terrain and without needing any kind of construction. This makes it easy for us to pick up and move the module whenever we want to move to some other place.

Since it is right in the middle of nature, the most important is that the home is well integrated with its surroundings. To this end they've put large windows, in fact, the whole front facade is made of glass. This maximizes the natural light coming in and makes the inside of the home that much more comfortable.

Thanks to its large windows you can better enjoy looking out at the landscape around the home. But this shouldn't keep us from having our moments of intimacy, which is why it's best to put some curtains whether they are classical (of fabric) or modern (of small boards).

Light colors must predominate on the walls because they reflect warmth and cleanness. Avoid dark colors because they are cold, even if they give a touch of modernity to a home.

Wee House > 334 sq. ft.

Geoffrey Warner/Alchemy Architects

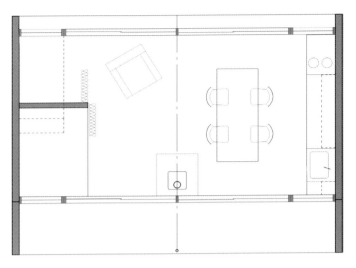

Floor plan

Getting away from the daily stress and rhythm of the city, and finding peace and quiet, are the goals we have to have in mind when building these small homes.

Just because it is built in the middle of nowhere, surrounded by nothing but nature, doesn't mean it can't have all the necessities. To maximize its 334 square feet it's been distributed on a single floor where the kitchen, living room and bedroom come together. Wood is the material most used because it gives a warm feel to the home, and we mustn't forget it connects it with its environment. Come time for decorating, homes that are removed from the city usually opt for a rustic style, but that doesn't mean that it's always better or more appropriate. This house is a good example. The owners opted for a more avant-garde décor, with a more modern design that renounces the classics.

Light is another of the primary factors in this construction. Since it doesn't have electricity, the architects chose to place some large windows that simultaneously serve as balconies on the two main facades. Doing this not only assures we enjoy the landscape, but also that the home's lighting is as good as possible during the day. At night, a woodburner placed in the center of the space gives us the light we need, as well as the heat that electric and oil heaters give us in the city.

Two cement pillars put the front of the house at the same level as the rear, which is resting on a small hill.

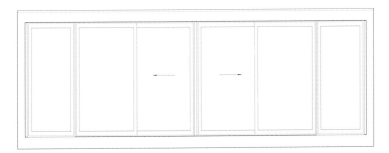

Elevation

Zenzmaier House

Maria Flöckner & Hermann Schnöll

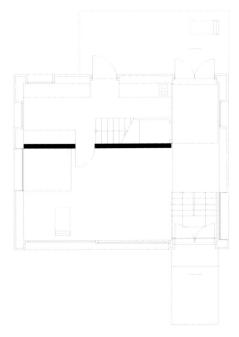

Floor plan

When building a home or an extension of the main home, you have to be very aware of your budget because this will determine not only its size but also its construction materials.

In this case they were looking for two independent homes that would also be independent of the main home. The first objective was to break away from the external structure of the main house. This was achieved and they also managed for the new additions to be perfectly integrated with their immediate environment.

As we said earlier, our budget is very important. Here they built two homes, so the budget for each of them was less. For this reason it was better to clearly set the amount necessary for the façade aside and then complement it with small touches of different materials that will give it a unique and personal touch. So here we are with three homes. Each independent of the others but, at the same time, connected: a stone pathway takes you from one to the other.

The architect has managed to create two homes that are different from the main one but have one thing in common: their contact with nature.

The materials were chosen and used intelligently. The resulting savings were invested in high quality siding with openings to the exterior.

Section

2parts House > 775 sq. ft.

Blanck Kosloff Knott Architects

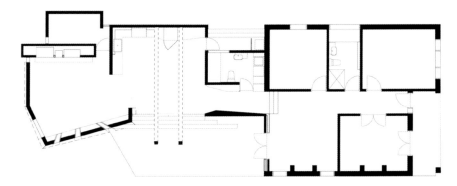

Floor plan

Here we have an example of a house extension that closely follows the structure, design and decor of the main house. It is a home characterized by being immersed in nature and for this reason the architect decided wood would make for the best structure to integrate it with its environment. The originality of this home lies in its windows, which stray away from conventional windows. In this case they are narrow openings that give the room a touch of dynamism.

As we said earlier, the architect tried to integrate the home with nature, and wood is the most appropriate material for this, but it is also important to decide on the best tone for finding what we're looking for. A light color, such as this one, is ideal because it not only makes the exterior lighter but it also makes its interior brighter. This brightness, combined with the light projected through the narrow windows, gives the home a warm and natural lighting.

But that intimate and personal touch isn't just achieved with the home's lighting and structure. Because it is in contact with nature, the best thing is to choose wood as a main element – this time combining different tones – for the floors and the furniture, without forgetting that come time for painting it's best to use white.

The imbalance produced by the structure isn't a problem when decorating since these days any piece of furniture can be made to measure and put anywhere you need.

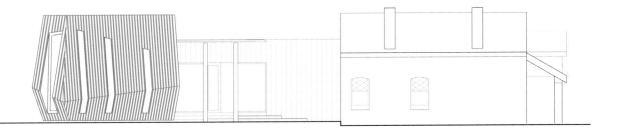

Section

Boat House > 377 sq. ft.

Drew Heath

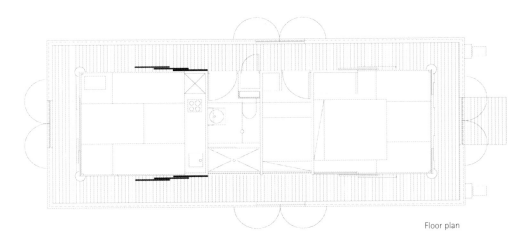

Floor plan

Enjoying some relaxing days away from the city is something we all wish for. A vacation at sea is a good choice so long as you like sailing, but that doesn't have to keep us from feeling perfectly at home. That's why they've created these kinds of homes, so we can have the comfort we normally have at home while enjoying our time for relaxation. We're looking at what could be called a floating house. A residence constructed according to our personal tastes and with the great advantage that we can enjoy it at each and every city we visit.

These houses have to be built upon a strong base, a base that we can cover however we like afterwards. It's best to make it of wood because it is a material that doesn't get slippery when wet. This base is complemented by one last important detail: you have to put a railing around the whole base so that the home is safe.

Wood panels predominate in construction, not just because they add warmth but also because wood is a light material. Windows are important for enjoying the landscape and making a place that is only 377 square feet seem bigger, while maximizing natural light as best we can.

A final detail with respect to its construction is the roof, which is made of a large sheet of metal. A sheet that is bigger than the home itself so that this way the whole structure of the home is protected.

Small spaces mean you have to look for practical solutions that are useful for maximizing the little space available.

Solar Box > 861 sq. ft.

Driendl Architects

Ground floor

Upon constructing this home, enjoying the landscape around the house was the architect's main objective and he achieved it. He created a space open to the outdoors, with large windows allowing one to see the entire yard and, at the same time, let as much natural light in as possible.

To do this it was best to use glass, a material that also gives an air of sophistication to a room. In this case the large windows we find on the four facades of the house stand out, letting one enjoy solar light throughout the whole day.

What complements glass best? Any material would do, but since we're looking to maximize the landscape, wood is the best option for the interior décor, as well as for the smaller details we want to be seen from the outside; and metal, more specifically, aluminum. This is the best material to put beside glass because together they contrast mutually.

This combination of materials, together with the stone used outside to cover the porch floor, makes for a modern look that adapts to the décor and its modern design without forgetting or leaving behind the architect's original aim: to enjoy the landscape around the house to the fullest.

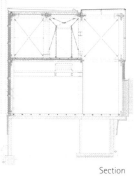

Section

*Besides letting in natural light, the large windows make it
so the home can be aired out easily.*

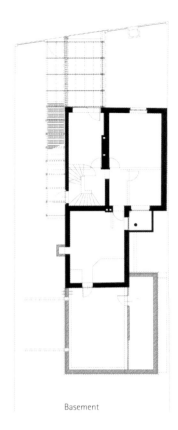

Basement

Upper floor

The home is divided in two floors. Downstairs is reserved for the common areas while upstairs you find private rooms such as the bedroom and bathroom.

Locher Apartment > 969 sq. ft.

Spoerri Tommen Architekten
© Michael Freisager Fotografie/Zurich, Switzerland

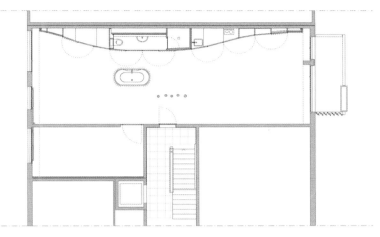

Floor plan

We're looking at a loft that is trying to put us in direct contact with nature. They achieve it thanks to the decor and the palette of colors used, but also thanks to the four tree trunks we find in the middle of the house. The house was built in the middle of nature and the architect has adapted to it, giving this house a unique touch because never before has a home had trunks that size in it for strictly decorative purposes.

But this isn't the only thing that calls your attention about this apartment. Until now we've been looking at walls that have been painted with light colors to add brightness – here they've achieved this as well – using wood to separate the different rooms. But now we're facing the perfect solution to help give a radical twist to our overall vision of a home: the use of fabric.

We find that the main partition, the first one we find upon opening the door, is upholstered with a green color that adds to the contact with nature that we were speaking about before, and gives it a touch of warmth and personality. But before upholstering we have to have one thing clear: you can't upholster a wall that has humidity, meaning you can't put fabric on bathroom and kitchen walls because these are rooms where water is used.

The upholstered wall contains the bathroom and kitchen.
These are two areas that are isolated from the other areas
that are used more for relaxation.

Hanse Colani Rotorhaus > 388 sq. ft.

Luigi Colani, Hanse Haus
© Hanse Haus GMBH/Oberleichtersbach, Germany

In this prefabricated house functional nature and design combine to create a futuristic home that has little to do with what we normally find.

The exterior breaks away from the structure of the main house. For starters, the walls aren't totally straight; they have a slight curve that gives it a touch of originality. A small detail that, in any case, fits perfectly with the atmosphere around the house because of the material used to cover the structure of the home: wood.

But what stands out most is what we find inside, where its décor and arrangement have nothing to do with what we've seen so far. Since it is a small home, the architect had to find a practical solution, that simultaneously suited the taste of those living there and covered their basic needs. To do this he decided to build a revolving cylinder divided into three areas – kitchen, bathroom and bedroom –, a cylinder that is controlled from the outside so the inhabitants can use each room whenever they like. This gives it an original touch, but at the same time, serves the purpose of having as many things as possible in a small space without overloading it. As far as the décor is concerned, a minimalist style is most appropriate, meaning to stray away from things that are good for nothing but to diminish the house's practicality.

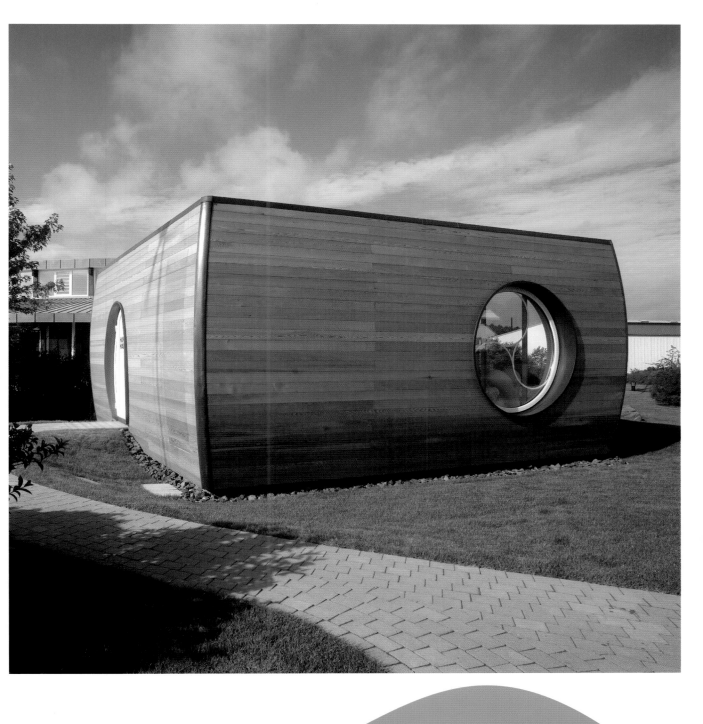

Since the interior of the home has a modern design, it's best to paint each small area with a different color. This heightens the contrast with the color of the walls, and hence, the brightness of the place.

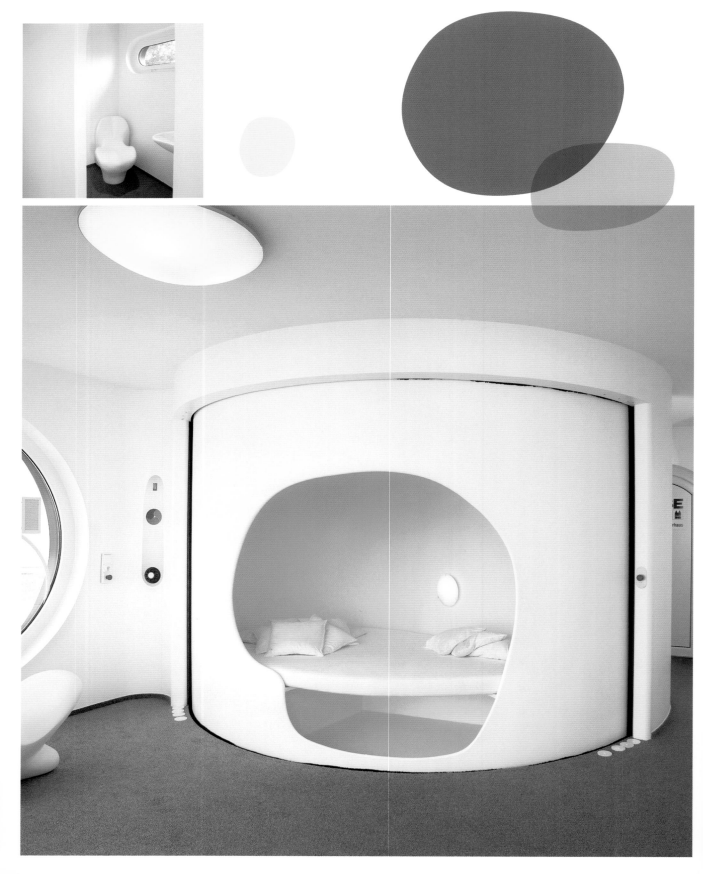

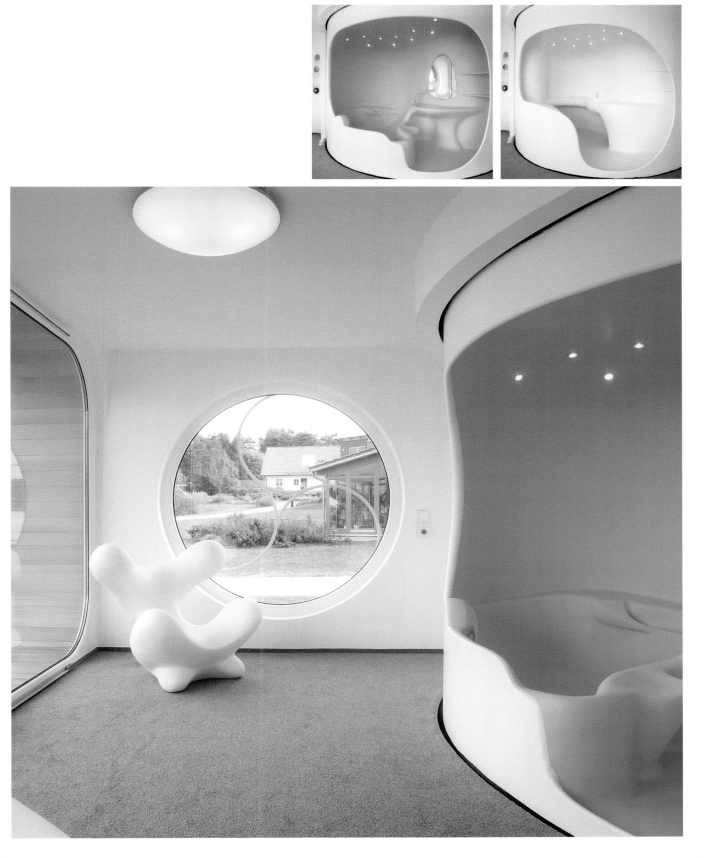

Study and Guesthouse > 1,141 sq. ft.

Loosen, Rüschoff & Winkler
© Oliver Heissner/Grossensee, Germany

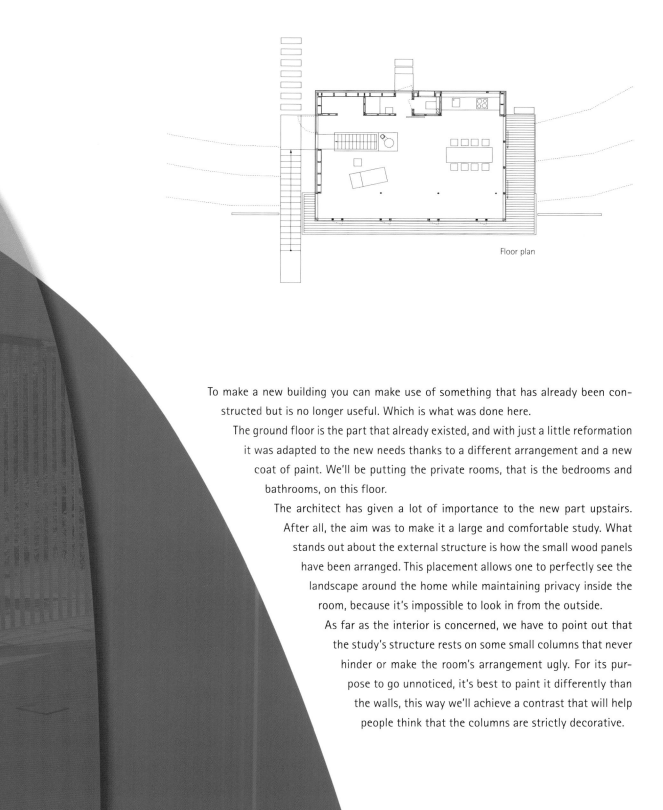

Floor plan

To make a new building you can make use of something that has already been constructed but is no longer useful. Which is what was done here.

The ground floor is the part that already existed, and with just a little reformation
it was adapted to the new needs thanks to a different arrangement and a new
coat of paint. We'll be putting the private rooms, that is the bedrooms and
bathrooms, on this floor.

The architect has given a lot of importance to the new part upstairs.
After all, the aim was to make it a large and comfortable study. What
stands out about the external structure is how the small wood panels
have been arranged. This placement allows one to perfectly see the
landscape around the home while maintaining privacy inside the
room, because it's impossible to look in from the outside.

As far as the interior is concerned, we have to point out that
the study's structure rests on some small columns that never
hinder or make the room's arrangement ugly. For its purpose to go unnoticed, it's best to paint it differently than
the walls, this way we'll achieve a contrast that will help
people think that the columns are strictly decorative.

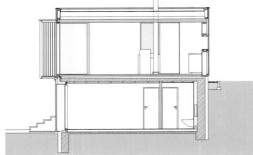

Section

The height of the study makes it so one can work in peace aided by the view outside the large windows.

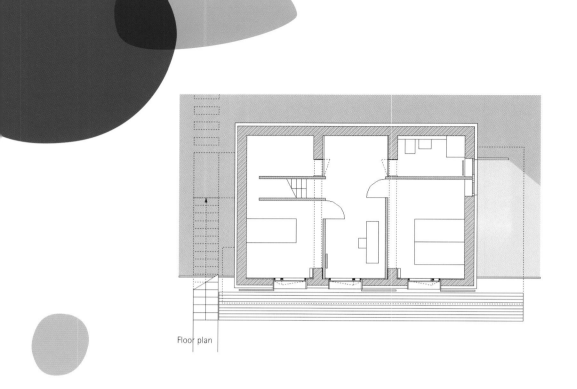

Floor plan

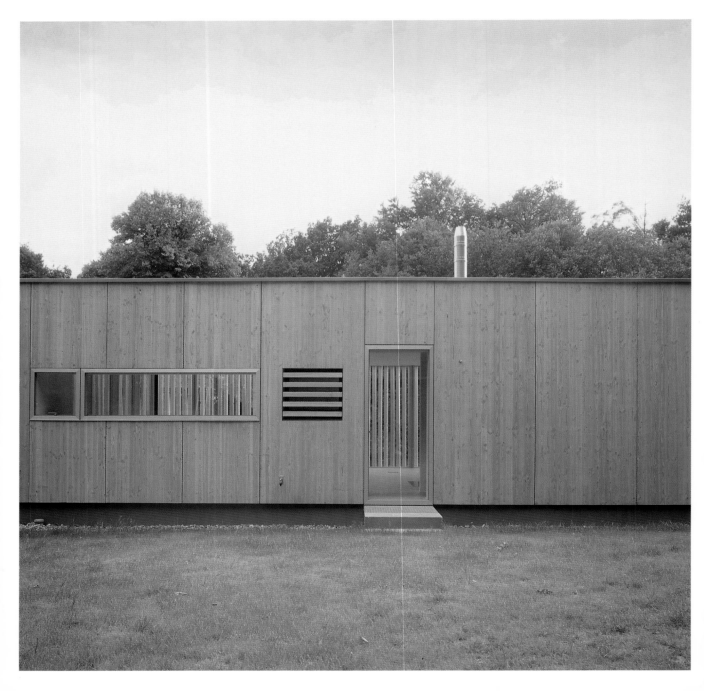

Dong Heon Residence > 710 sq. ft.

Seung H-Sang/Iroje Architects & Planners
© Muari Osamu/Namyangju-Gun, Korea

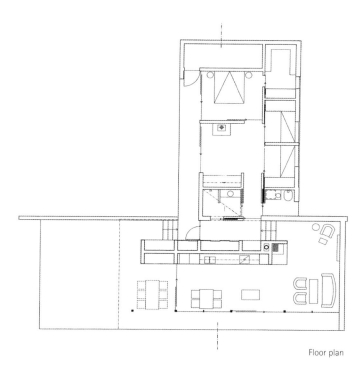

Floor plan

Why can we find a small home in the middle of nowhere? Thanks to modern design evolving with the passing of time, space and all the other elements it comes across along the way.

That's how the house we are looking at now can be explained. It has had no trouble adapting to nature, as the architect chose an L shape to avoid touching any existing elements.

What stands out about this house is that its entire structure is made of steel, a material that is being used more and more frequently. Its high resistance compared to its weight mean that the structure as a whole weighs less. This is why the architect chose steel, because it is ideal for constructions where building a foundation is complicated.

In addition, you have to take into account that steel is one of the most resistant materials, withstanding all sorts of inclement weather and practically all of the elements. It's resistant to termites, fungus, rodents and is able to withstand temperatures of 752 °F. In short, it is a material that makes for a very secure home.

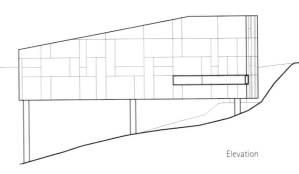

Elevation

The pillars supporting the structure allow the home to adapt to its surroundings. A landscape that can be enjoyed thanks to the large windows complementing the steel.

Layer House > 355 sq. ft.

Hiroaki Ohtani
© Kouji Okamoto/Kobe, Japan

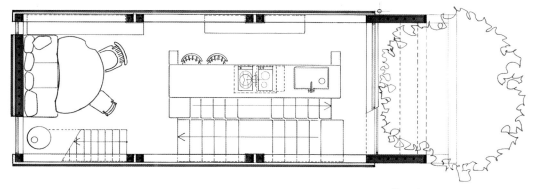

Floor plan

The high demand for apartments over the last few years, combined with prices easily exceeding our wildest imaginations, has completely changed the concept of housing as we knew it. It seems almost impossible for us to live in just 355 square feet, but thanks to modern design, we can manage to have all our daily basic necessities fit into such a reduced space.

Cities aren't big enough to satisfy the existing demand so it's normal that in places like Japan, where there are almost 130 million inhabitants, finding quick and practical solutions becomes a must. The Layer House is a good example. It may not seem very livable when seen from the outside, but this first impression dissipates quickly when you look at its interior distribution. It is innovative in the sense that rarely has wood been used as the basic structure for organizing a house. It's a material that lends warmth to a room and, at the same time, gives us the light we need. The distribution of the wood should be strategic so as to maximize the large windows. We have to let natural light come in, giving the small room a more personal touch. Lastly, there are no rules to follow when it comes to distributing space. The Layer House is divided into three floors, but what we put on each floor depends on the person who will be living there.

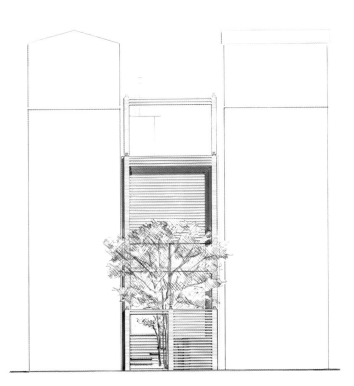

Elevation

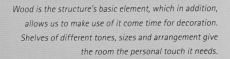

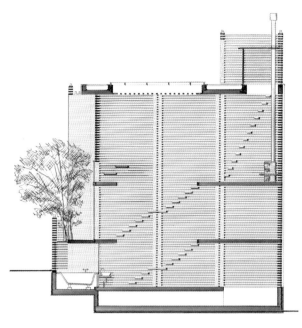

Section

Chelsea Apartment > 570 sq. ft.

Rafael Berkowitz/RB Architects
© James Wilkins/New York, United States

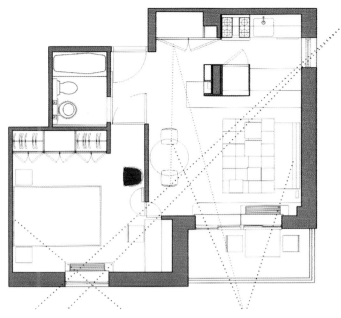

Floor plan

Having a small home doesn't mean we have to forget about all those elements that we feel are essential in our lives, nor must we sacrifice our decorative taste. Fortunately, design has evolved over the years and today it adapts well to all styles and needs.

In the first place, you have to be fully conscious of the space you're dealing with and then decide what kind of decor and furniture to use. You have to seek simple lines that make better use of space while adding towards our personal comfort. The best way of doing this is to order made to measure furniture. These are pieces of furniture that adapt to any corner of the house and which, in addition, meet our tastes and needs. For example, if we focus on the bedroom, the best thing is to put built-in closets to maximize space.

As far as colors are concerned, you have to avoid very dark colors. We mustn't forget that in small homes the most important thing is to find the lighting that will make the home look larger, and the windows are one of the most important elements in this respect. Despite this, some hints of bright color will personalize a home and give it a modern and original touch. Lastly, it's best to avoid useless things when decorating. Add small details that don't take up much space but which, at the same, lend personality to the place.

Being able to use a space for various different purposes – in this case, the tiny study within the main bedroom – lets us improve the home's functional nature while giving it a more modern feel.

Kang Duplex > 1,399 sq. ft.

Shi-chieh Lu/CJ Studio

© Kuomin Lee/Taipei, Taiwan

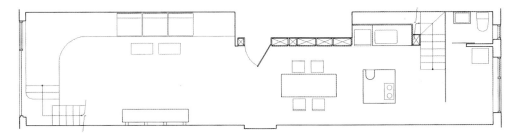

Ground floor

You have to make the most of what a space has to offer. That's the premise the architect was after when designing this home and laying out its rooms. One of the main advantages in this case is that the house has various large windows that you'll find in the most important rooms: in the living room, which allows us to admire the landscape around the house from the inside, in addition to improving the use of natural light; the kitchen, the area of the house that needs the best ventilation to avoid smoke and bad odors; and the bedroom, which also includes a mini-study.

But light and spaciousness in a room isn't only achieved thanks to the solar light coming in through the big windows. The color used for the walls is also key. In this case they chose a simple color that never fails: white. It's a color that predominates throughout the house, even on the stairs going upstairs, because it gives unity to the structure of the home.

Lastly, another of the elements that give this home its special touch are the stairs, which aren't at all conventional. The steps aren't interconnected, adding depth to the room and its main advantage is that it doesn't break or obstruct the natural light coming through the windows since the stairs were planned to adapt to the structure created by the architect.

The elongated and narrow surface area of the space was given a makeover by introducing a frosted glass panel on the rear façade and painting the walls and ceiling in white to generate continuity and luminosity.

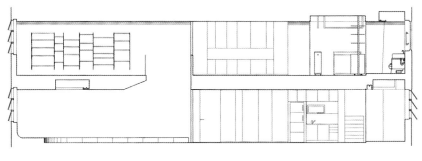

Section

Zig Zag Cabin > 269 sq. ft.

Drew Heath
© Brett Boardman/Wollombi, Australia

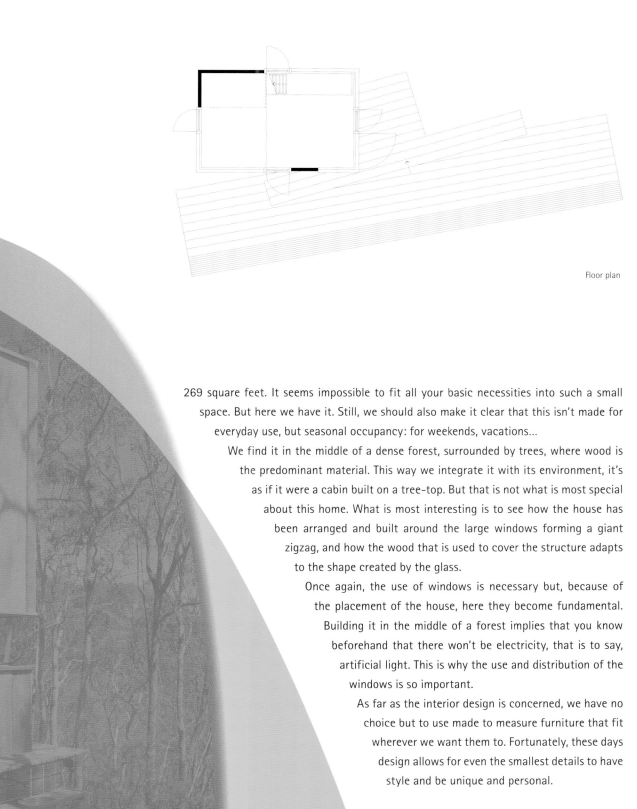

Floor plan

269 square feet. It seems impossible to fit all your basic necessities into such a small space. But here we have it. Still, we should also make it clear that this isn't made for everyday use, but seasonal occupancy: for weekends, vacations...

We find it in the middle of a dense forest, surrounded by trees, where wood is the predominant material. This way we integrate it with its environment, it's as if it were a cabin built on a tree-top. But that is not what is most special about this home. What is most interesting is to see how the house has been arranged and built around the large windows forming a giant zigzag, and how the wood that is used to cover the structure adapts to the shape created by the glass.

Once again, the use of windows is necessary but, because of the placement of the house, here they become fundamental. Building it in the middle of a forest implies that you know beforehand that there won't be electricity, that is to say, artificial light. This is why the use and distribution of the windows is so important.

As far as the interior design is concerned, we have no choice but to use made to measure furniture that fit wherever we want them to. Fortunately, these days design allows for even the smallest details to have style and be unique and personal.

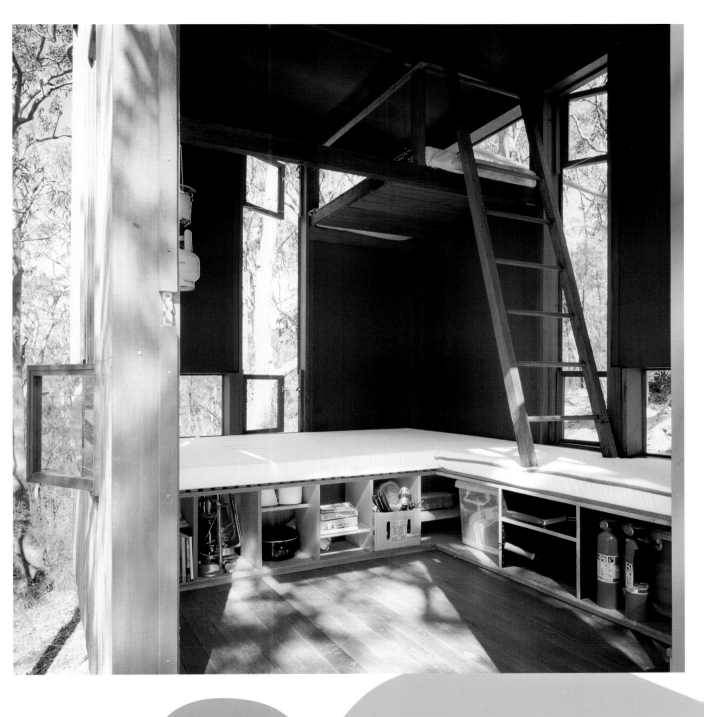

The views you can see through the large windows fulfill the purpose for which the home was built: for the inhabitants' well-being and relaxation.

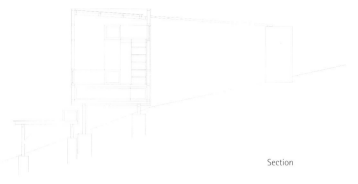

Section

Natural Wedge > 915 sq. ft.

Masaki Endoh
© Luis Paulsen Lighting A/S/Tokyo, Japan

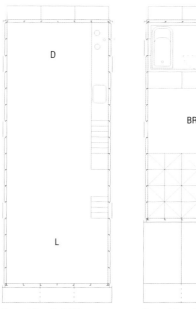

D

BTH

BR

L

Ground floor S=1:150   Second floor S=1:150

Floor plan

Design has evolved over the years, encouraging interior home design to improve and adapt to the passing of time, the emerging decorative styles, and especially to our individual personal tastes.

But fortunately, design has also little by little become more visible in the external aspects of home construction: in terms of structures and facades. This is the case of Natural Wedge. It is a triangular structure, basically made of metal, but since this is a pretty cold material, they decided to counterbalance it by putting various windows and a large window on one side of the house. Why? Because glass is a material that, without us noticing it, adds a touch of distinction to a home. In addition to helping air out small spaces, it allows one to enjoy natural light to the fullest.

If we step inside the home we'll see how the intertwined metal structure on the ceiling and the steel panels covering the walls stand out. As we said earlier, metal can come across as cold, but we can avoid this by playing with light colors. The walls are pastel green which combined with the natural and artificial light lend warmth to the room.

Mixing natural and artificial light allows to play with light
in a way that would be much more difficult in homes
with a different structure, giving it a very unique and
personal touch.

The triangular structure changes the size of the rooms
considerably. Thus the ground floor, which will be larger,
could be used for the living room, and the upstairs can be
used for more private areas such as the bedroom.

Elevation